Published in 2015 by The Rosen Publishing Group, Inc.
29 East 21st Street, New York, NY 10010

Photo Credits: **Key** tl=top left; tc=top center; tr=top right; cl=center left; c=center; b=bottom; bl=bottom left; bc=bottom center; br=bottom right; bg=background

CBT = Corbis; GI = Getty Images; iS = istockphoto.com; PDCD = PhotoDisc; SH = Shutterstock; TF = Topfoto; TPL = photolibrary.com

6–7bg PDCD; **7**br TPL; **8**bl, tl iS; **10–11**b iS; **15**tc SH; **16**c CBT; **18**cl GI; **18–19**bg PDCD; **19**br iS; **20**cl iS; **21**tr iS; **22**cl SH; **22–23**bg PDCD; **23**cl TF; **24**cl CBT; **25**tl CBT; bc, br TF; **26**tr TPL; **27**bc iS; **28**cl iS; **28–29**bg PDCD; **30–31**bg PDCD

All illustrations copyright Weldon Owen Pty Ltd, except **20–21**c Magic Group.
16tl; **20**tl; **22**tl; **24**tl Andrew Davies/Creative Communication; **22**br; **23**bl, br Gary Hanna

WELDON OWEN PTY LTD
Managing Director: Kay Scarlett
Creative Director: Sue Burk
Publisher: Helen Bateman
Senior Vice President, International Sales: Stuart Laurence
Vice President Sales North America: Ellen Towell
Administration Manager, International Sales: Kristine Ravn

Library of Congress Cataloging-in-Publication Data

Coupe, Robert, author.
 Cats of the wild / by Robert Coupe.
    pages cm. — (Discovery education. Animals)
 Includes index.
 ISBN 978-1-4777-6944-7 (library binding) — ISBN 978-1-4777-6945-4 (pbk.) —
ISBN 978-1-4777-6946-1 (6-pack)
 1. Felidae—Juvenile literature. 2. Rare animals—Juvenile literature. 3. Endangered species—
Juvenile literature. I. Title.
 QL737.C23C6785 2015
 599.75—dc23

Manufactured in the United States of America

CPSIA Compliance Information: Batch #WS14PK3: For Further Information contact Rosen Publishing, New York, New York at 1-800-237-9932

ANIMALS

CATS OF THE WILD

Robert Coupe

PowerKiDS press.

New York

Contents

What Is a Cat?

Pet cats are usually tame, affectionate animals, but they are members of a large family of cats—and all of them are natural hunters.

Most cats eat only meat, and many hunt their prey at night. A pet cat will crouch quietly, then spring suddenly to catch a fly or another insect, or even a mouse, in its sharp claws. That is how all cats hunt. Big cats, such as lions, tigers, cheetahs, and leopards, catch and feed on much larger prey.

The skeleton

The bone structure of most cats is very similar. It varies from one species to another mainly according to size and diet. The hind legs are longer than the front legs, which enables cats to jump long distances.

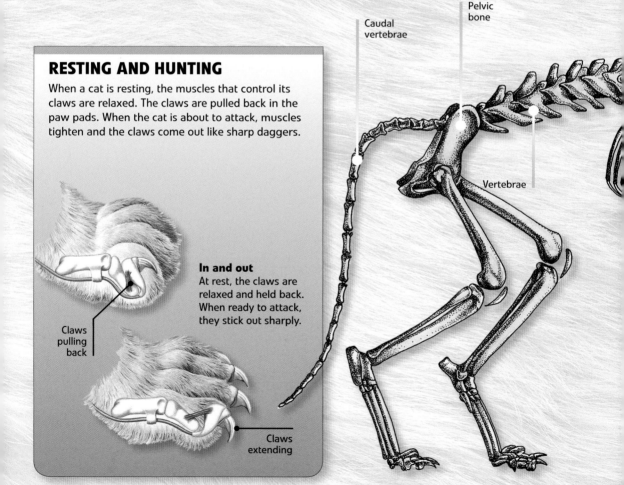

RESTING AND HUNTING

When a cat is resting, the muscles that control its claws are relaxed. The claws are pulled back in the paw pads. When the cat is about to attack, muscles tighten and the claws come out like sharp daggers.

In and out
At rest, the claws are relaxed and held back. When ready to attack, they stick out sharply.

Claws pulling back

Claws extending

Caudal vertebrae

Pelvic bone

Vertebrae

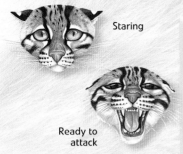

Staring

Ready to attack

Attack and defense

A margay stares at an enemy to frighten it away. If that does not work, it opens its mouth and prepares to attack.

A rough tongue

If a cat licks your hand, its tongue feels rough. This is because the tongue is covered with tiny bumps, like the ends of hooks. These tips are called papillae.

Papillae

The rough papillae on the tongue are used for cleaning a cat's fur. They also help to scrape meat off the bones of prey.

Papillae

Skull

Scapula

Ribs

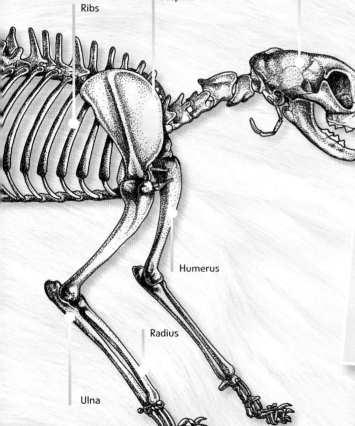

Humerus

Radius

Ulna

Did You Know?

Wild cats are found on all continents except Antarctica and Australia. There are 36 species of wild cats and many species live on only one continent.

Smilodon

This ancient cat, *Smilodon fatalis*, with its two huge saber teeth, lived until about 10,000 years ago. It must have been a fierce hunter.

Lions

Except for tigers, lions are the largest of the big cats. They are, in many ways, typical mammals. Their bodies are covered with fur, they travel in groups to find food, and they care for their young and feed them with milk.

Adult male lions have a mane of bushy hair around their head. Females, which are smaller than males, have no mane. Lionesses nurse their offspring, called cubs, for up to six months.

Where they live
Most lions live on grassy plains in Africa. A small number live in western India.

The mane event
A male lion's mane is fully grown at about five years old. At first it is golden in color, but becomes darker and browner as the lion grows older.

1 Starting the hunt
A lioness springs into action in pursuit of a fleeing antelope, always increasing her speed.

Whiskers
Like all cats, lions have a keen sense of smell. They also use their whiskers to sense and identify objects and other animals that are nearby. The whiskers can point forward when the lion senses something straight ahead.

Lioness on the hunt
Groups of lionesses do most of the hunting, while males stand guard against intruders. Working in numbers helps them trap the fast-moving animals, such as antelope or zebra, that are their favorite prey.

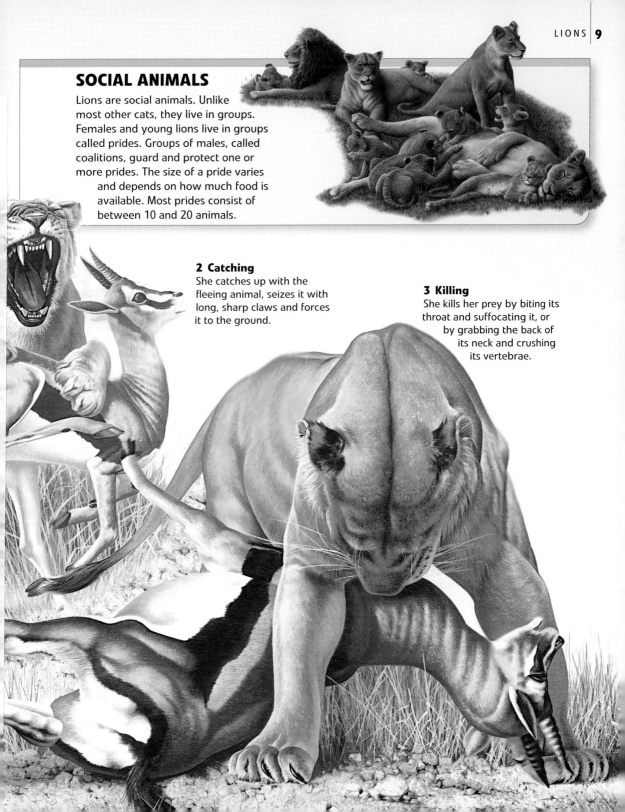

SOCIAL ANIMALS

Lions are social animals. Unlike most other cats, they live in groups. Females and young lions live in groups called prides. Groups of males, called coalitions, guard and protect one or more prides. The size of a pride varies and depends on how much food is available. Most prides consist of between 10 and 20 animals.

2 Catching
She catches up with the fleeing animal, seizes it with long, sharp claws and forces it to the ground.

3 Killing
She kills her prey by biting its throat and suffocating it, or by grabbing the back of its neck and crushing its vertebrae.

Tigers

Where they live
Tigers live in many parts of Asia, including India, Nepal, Myanmar, Thailand, Bangladesh, Vietnam, Russia, and China. Tigers living in hot places are darker in color.

You could never mistake a tiger. Among the 36 members of the cat family, tigers are the only big cats with stripes. They are the largest of the big cats. The largest tiger, the Siberian tiger, grows up to 12 feet (3.7 m) long and can weigh more than 700 pounds (318 kg).

Tigers live in many types of environments, from cold, snow-covered forests of Russia and northern China to hot, tropical forests, and even swamps. They need to live near water and are very good swimmers.

The white tiger has creamy white fur with dark stripes. It is seldom seen in the wild but can be seen in several zoos.

On the attack

These fierce hunters have large appetites, and need to catch large prey. They make long leaps, but can run fast only over short distances. They use cunning and stealth to creep up on and trap their victims, which include deer, pigs, and buffalo. They will also attack and kill humans.

Solitary life

Tigers are solitary animals. They usually live alone and hunt at night. Two or more tigers may come together to share a meal that one has caught. Adult females spend much of their lives caring for their young.

Teeth and jaws

A tiger's sharp teeth, wide gape, and powerful jaws deliver a deadly bite, usually to the front or back of a victim's neck. At the front of the mouth are long, sharp canine teeth and shorter incisors. Farther back are the molars and premolars that can strip meat from bones.

Canine

Molar

Incisor

Unseen stalker

The stripes and golden-yellow coat are excellent camouflage. They allow the tiger to blend in with forest vegetation or long grass as it silently edges closer to its intended meal.

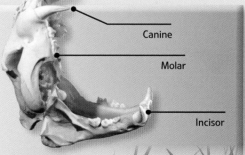

Where they live
Leopards live throughout most of central and southern Africa, and in many parts of Asia.

Leopards

Tigers have their stripes and leopards have their spots, but these spots differ greatly between species. Leopards are much smaller than tigers, but are strong and agile enough to catch and kill very large prey, as well as smaller victims, such as birds, snakes, and fish. They are expert tree climbers and also good swimmers.

Leopards have the widest distribution of all the big cats. This is partly because they can eat a very wide variety of prey.

LEOPARD SPOTS

We say that leopards have spots, but they are not really spots at all. They are, in fact, small dark circles or rosettes. Jaguars, too, have rosettes rather than genuine spots.

Hard to see
A leopard's markings make it hard to see against the tree branches on which it rests, watching for prey below.

Clouded leopard
It is easy to see where this leopard gets its name, as its markings are different from other leopards. It lives in the warm forests of Southeast Asia and hunts monkeys, birds, and larger prey. Its incisor teeth are very long—almost as long as a lion's.

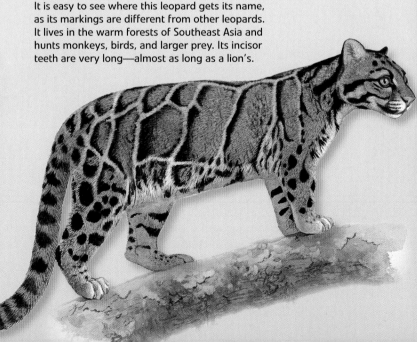

Black panther
Some leopards are very dark colored. They are often called black panthers. But they are real leopards. Like all leopards, they have spots, but they are very hard to see against the animal's dark coat.

Time to eat
High up in the fork of a tree, a leopard starts its meal.

Super-size serving
A large warthog makes a filling meal for an agile leopard.

Undisturbed meal

This leopard in Africa has killed a warthog on the ground and dragged it by the throat up to a high tree branch. It has draped its prey over the branch and can now eat it, without having to compete with lions, hyenas, or other predators.

Jaguars

After tigers and lions, jaguars are the third largest of the big cats. Most jaguars have golden coats with distinctive black markings. They are natural forest dwellers, but can also live in some grassland and semidesert areas.

Jaguars are expert climbers and swimmers, and often hunt fish and other aquatic animals in rivers, lakes, and streams. They often prey on large land animals that feed in water. They can swim for long distances, carrying their prey in their mouth.

Where they live
Jaguars are restricted to parts of Central and South America.

Watching for prey
Jaguars climb forest trees and lie in wait for prey below. They prefer larger animals and only rarely spring down to catch small prey. The jaguar's markings blend with forest colors, and make it hard to see them.

Black jaguars
Some forest panthers are black all over. They are almost impossible to see in the forest shadows and are lethal hunters.

Coat patterns
Most jaguars have golden coats that are covered with large black spots and spots surrounded by black circles. No two jaguars have exactly the same coat markings.

FIERCE PREDATORS

Jaguars prey on many animals but, unlike leopards, they rarely attack humans. They often kill their victims by crushing their head with their powerful canine teeth. They are the only big cats to kill in this way. They can even cut through the tough shells of river turtles.

Anteaters are prey to jaguars.

A jaguar sits perched and ready to strike.

Sharp sight

Jaguars hunt mainly at night. They see up to seven times more clearly than humans can in the dark.

Deadly teeth

A jaguar uses its long canine teeth to kill prey. The shorter teeth are also very sharp. They can crush bones and hold or chew up meat.

In dense forests

Jaguars are larger than the other cats that roam in the dense forests of Central and South America. They are solitary predators that hunt by stalking and ambushing.

Jaguars eat pythons and anacondas.

Snow Leopards

S now leopards are a different species from other leopards. They are smaller than other leopards and have silvery-gray fur that is covered with spots or rosettes. Their coloring helps camouflage them against the snowy, rocky mountain environment in which they live.

With their very thick fur, snow leopards are well adapted to cold conditions. They prey on sheep, deer, and smaller animals, such as birds and hares.

Where they live
Snow leopards live in steep, rocky mountain areas in central Asia. They are sparsely distributed in parts of Russia, Mongolia, China, Nepal, and India.

Endangered
Fewer than 10,000 snow leopards are now estimated to live in the wild, although many have been bred successfully in captivity. In the past, they were hunted for their thick fur, and have lost much of their natural habitat as human settlements expanded into their range.

RAISING CUBS

Male and female snow leopards mate during the winter. About three months later, in the milder spring weather, two or three, or even as many as five, cubs are born. After about three months, the cubs follow their mother when she goes hunting. At the age of two, the cubs are ready to go out on their own.

Very young cubs live in a rocky den that is lined with their mother's fur.

Well adapted

A snow leopard has wide, flat paws that help prevent it from sinking into the snow as it prowls in search of prey. Its long, thick tail helps it to keep balance as it leaps from one rock to the next in the rugged mountain terrain.

Unlike most other big cats, snow leopards cannot roar. They can, however, make mewing and wailing sounds.

Pumas

Pumas are one of only two big cats that do not have spots, stripes, or other markings on their fur. The other is the African lion. Coat color varies according to the puma's habitat, which ranges from very cold areas to hot and tropical regions throughout the Americas. They live in tropical forests, pine forests, swamps, and on grassy plains, from sea level to mountain altitudes of almost 15,000 feet (4,573 m). Pumas hunt a wide variety of prey, from deer and horses to small animals, such as hares and porcupines.

Where they live
Pumas live in South and Central America, and in parts of the western US and Canada.

An endangered species
The Florida panther is a special kind of puma that now lives only in swamps in Florida. They once had a wider range, but hunting and destruction of their habitat have reduced their numbers to fewer than one hundred.

Five-lined lizard

Raccoon

Powerful paws
Pumas use their large, powerful front paws to trap their prey. This puma is about to pounce on a raccoon. The raccoon is too busy catching a lizard to notice the puma's approach.

Different colors
Adult pumas have plain-colored coats, but puma cubs have spots, which fade as they grow. In hot areas, they tend to have reddish-yellow coats. In cold northern regions, their coats are generally a grayish color.

ATHLETIC ANIMAL

Pumas, which are also known as mountain lions and cougars, have long bodies and very strong back legs. They can leap long distances and can spring up to 15 feet (4.6 m) onto tree branches or rock ledges. Their long tail helps to balance them as they run after prey.

Pumas often hide in bushes and sneak up on their prey.

Cheetahs

These spotted, swift-moving big cats live in the savanna grasslands of Africa, and compete for prey with larger lions and leopards. They hunt during the day for animals smaller than themselves, such as gazelles, impala, young wildebeest, and hares.

Cheetahs have very keen eyesight and often seek out their prey from mounds and other elevated positions. They have small heads, long, lean bodies, and long tails.

Where they live
Cheetahs live in open, grassy areas in Africa. A very small number live in Iran.

Land-speed record
Cheetahs can run faster than any other land animal. They reach speeds of up to 68 miles (110 km) per hour, but only over short distances.

Male cheetahs
Males from the same litter sometimes stay together in a group. Males from different litters may also join up so they can defend their territory more easily.

Accelerating
As it springs into action, a cheetah needs only 2.5 seconds to reach a speed of 45 miles (72 km) per hour. From there it accelerates to its top speed.

Pushing from back feet

Landing on front feet

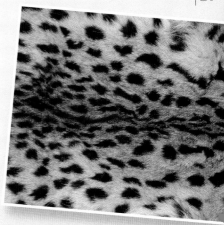

"King" cheetah
So-called "king" cheetahs are the same species as other cheetahs, but their fur is longer and darker, and spots on their back join up to form long stripes.

Many spots
The spots on cheetahs are real, solid spots. Leopards and jaguars have spots, but they are really small rosettes.

Female cheetahs
Females usually give birth to a litter of three to five cubs, though some litters have up to eight cubs. The females hunt to feed their young, and defend them against lions and other predators.

Young cheetahs
Many young cheetahs do not survive to become adults. They are killed by predators and others starve when their mother is unable to catch enough food for them.

Cheetahs do not roar. Instead, they make a kind of high-pitched howling sound.

Back feet again pushing forward

Front feet thrusting out

Bobcats, Lynxes, and Caracals

Lynxes and bobcats are closely related small- and medium-sized cats. Their habitats range from cold, snowy mountains to forests and even deserts. They all have tufts of hair at their ear tips, wide paws, and short tails. Lynxes have sharp hearing and good smell.

Where they live
Bobcats live in North America, from southern Canada to Mexico. Lynxes and caracals live in North America, Europe, Asia, and parts of Africa.

Caracals
Closely related to the lynx, caracals live throughout Africa and parts of Asia in dry woodland and mountain areas. They feed on small animals, such as mice and birds, but can also catch small deer.

Bobcats
These North American animals are about twice the size of an average adult pet cat. Rabbits and hares are their favorite food.

CATCHING DINNER

Bobcats live mainly on a diet of rabbits and hares, but they also catch rodents, such as muskrats, and birds, snakes, and even small deer. These pictures show how a bobcat approaches a muskrat, grabs it in its front paws, then kills it. Its meal is then ready to eat.

1 Stalking
The bobcat has seen, smelt, or heard the muskrat moving. It moves in to stalk it.

North American lynxes
These look like bobcats. They are gray or light brown, with faint spots, and their tails have a black tip. They live in the northern US, Canada, and Alaska.

Eurasian lynxes
Almost twice as big as bobcats, Eurasian lynxes have clear, dark spots and live mostly in forests in Europe and parts of Asia. They feed on rabbits and hares.

Spanish lynxes
The Spanish lynx lives in parts of Spain and Portugal. It is similar to the Eurasian lynx, but is smaller and has darker spots. It likes to eat rabbits.

2 Catching
The bobcat grabs the muskrat in its front paws, flips it over, then catches it again.

3 Killing
Holding the muskrat in its front paws, the bobcat kills it with a bite to the front of its neck.

Ocelots, Servals, and Margays

Where they live
Ocelots and margays live in northern South America and in Central America. Servals live in central and southern Africa.

argays live in rain forests and are the most skillful of all cat climbers. They feed mainly on birds that they often catch high up in trees. Ocelots also live in rain forests, but their habitat also includes dry forests and scrubby country. While these animals are widespread in South and Central America, the serval hunts rodents, birds, and other small prey on the open grasslands of central and southern Africa.

Giving birth
Female ocelots produce litters of only one or two kittens. These are born in a den that is well hidden from possible predators. The newborn kittens have almost the same markings as adult cats.

Colorful coat
Ocelots are medium-sized cats with small, rounded ears. Along their back and sides are long, open spots that are paler in the middle.

An ocelot catches a bird.

A VARIED DIET
An ocelot's diet is quite a varied one. It hunts on the ground at night in areas where there is plenty of cover, mainly for rodents and small mammals. Ocelots are good climbers and swimmers, and also catch fish, birds, lizards, and snakes.

Growing quickly
Only seven months after it is born, a young serval is as big as its mother. Two or three young servals are born in a litter.

Standing tall
A serval is a tall cat with large ears and very sharp hearing. These cats hunt small prey and can leap high to catch birds.

Fur coats
Until quite recently, ocelots and margays were widely hunted for their skins, which were made into fur coats. As a result, their numbers declined dramatically. Hunting of these cats is now illegal.

Look-alike margay
A margay looks a lot like an ocelot, but it is much smaller. With very sharp claws, it can grip tree branches, and can even hang upside down from them.

Margay fur beret

Other Wild Cats

While habitat loss and human activities, such as hunting and expanding settlements, have reduced the numbers of some animals, there is still a wonderful variety of cat species that survive in the wild in many parts of the world today.

Jaguarundi
This strange-looking cat is only about as big as a large domestic cat. It lives in Central and South America.

African golden cat
Living in western and central Africa, this cat may have a plain or a spotted coat. It is about twice the size of an average domestic cat.

African wild cat
This cat lives throughout most of Africa, and feeds mainly on rodents. It often comes close to towns and can be tamed.

Fishing cat

WEBBED PAWS

The fishing cat lives in wetland areas throughout parts of southern and southwest Asia. Its front toes are partially webbed and it can use its front paws to scoop fish out of streams. It sometimes wades into shallow water. As well as fish, it feeds on birds and small mammals.

Kodkod
Now rare, this cat lives only in parts of Chile and Argentina. It is about the size of a small domestic cat.

Did You Know?

The African golden cat shares its habitat and range with the much larger leopard, and so it is often called the "leopard's brother."

Asian golden cat
This cat lives mainly in forests in parts of north and Southeast Asia. Its color is often golden, but it can also be dark brown or even gray.

European wild cat
Also known as the forest wild cat, this cat is widely scattered through Europe. It looks like a domestic tabby cat.

Jungle cat
Because it has such a wide distribution, from Southeast Asia through central Asia and into Egypt, this cat varies greatly in size and color, and eats a wide variety of prey.

Spanish lynx

This is the most endangered of all cats. It now exists in only a small area in Spain and Portugal. As its favorite prey, rabbits, have declined in numbers, it has had to compete more and more with foxes for other prey. It is a battle the lynxes are losing.

Tiger

This superb animal has long been hunted for its skin, or simply for sport. A century ago, there were about 100,000 tigers in the wild. Today, only about 2,500 breeding adults remain.

Asian lion

The Asian lion is smaller than its African cousin. Less than 400 of these lions now survive, and they all live in the Gir National Park in Gujurat, western India. They once ranged widely through parts of the Middle East and northern India.

Endangered Cats

When a kind of animal disappears completely, we say that it is extinct. When the numbers of a species decline sharply or become very low, we say that that animal is endangered. Throughout the world's history, many animals have become extinct. Sometimes this happens through natural causes, but, especially in recent years, human activity is largely to blame.

Today, a number of wild cats are endangered. Some have been hunted almost out of existence. Others have had their habitat greatly reduced as human populations expand and towns, farms, and other settlements take over their territory.

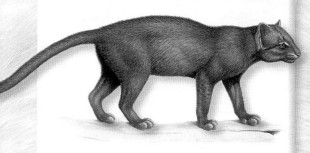

Andean cat

As its name suggests, this cat lives high up in a very limited area of the Andes Mountains in South America. It is so rare and isolated that very little is known about how it lives. Numbers seem to be declining as the prey in its rugged habitat has become rarer.

Jaguarundi

In some parts of its range throughout Central and South America, expanding human activities have destroyed much of this cat's habitat. It is now rare in some regions, especially in Mexico. It is also still widely hunted in some countries.

About 10,000 years ago, at the end of the last ice age, cheetahs became almost extinct. Today's cheetahs have descended from the few who survived at that time.

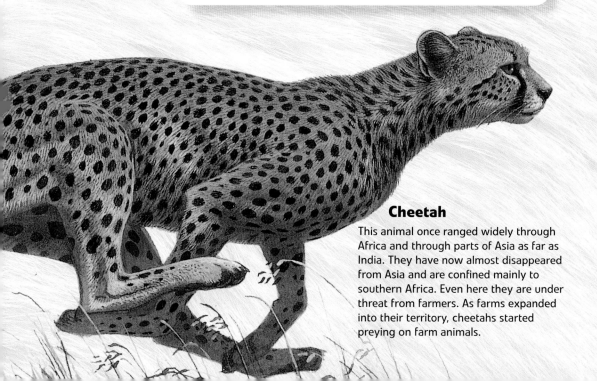

Cheetah

This animal once ranged widely through Africa and through parts of Asia as far as India. They have now almost disappeared from Asia and are confined mainly to southern Africa. Even here they are under threat from farmers. As farms expanded into their territory, cheetahs started preying on farm animals.

Glossary

adapted
(uh-DAPT-ed)
Describes an animal that is
able to live successfully in its
environment and find the
things it needs to survive.

ambushing
(AM-bush-ing)
Lying in wait in a hidden
place and then springing out
and attacking suddenly.

aquatic (uh-KWAH-tik)
Describes an animal that lives
entirely or partly in water.
Frogs are aquatic animals.

camouflage
(KA-muh-flahj) Colors and
patterns on an animal's body
that help it to blend in with
its surroundings and make it
hard to see.

canine teeth
(KAY-nyn TEATH)
Long, pointed teeth near the
front of a mammal's mouth.
Many predators use canine
teeth to catch and kill
their prey.

coalition
(koh-uh-LIH-shun)
A number of male lions that
live together in a group.
Coalitions of lions protect
groups of females and
lion cubs.

cubs (KUBZ) The young
of big cats and of some
other animals, such as bears
and foxes.

den (DEN) A covered,
hidden place where an
animal can take shelter and
hide from danger.

endangered
(in-DAYN-jerd)
Describes a species of animal
of which all members are in
danger of dying out.

extinct (ik-STINGKT)
Describes animals that once
existed but no longer exists.

habitat (HA-buh-tat) The
kind of environment in which
an animal lives in the wild,
such as a forest, a desert,
a river, or a part of the
ocean. A habitat provides the
animal with the food, shelter,
and other things that it
needs to survive.

humerus (HYOO-muh-rus)
The upper bone in an
animal's front leg. The
humerus joins the shoulder
to the lower leg.

incisor teeth
(in-SY-zur TEATH)
The front teeth, in the upper
and lower jaws of humans

and other mammals,
between the longer and
sharper canine teeth. Incisor
teeth are used for cutting
through food.

lethal (LEE-thul) Extremely
dangerous and likely to
cause death.

litter (LIH-ter) A number of
young animals that have the
same mother and that are
born at the same time.

mammal
(MA-mul) A warm-blooded
animal that has a backbone
and hair on its body, and that
feeds its young on milk from
its body. Humans are
mammals. So are dogs, cats,
seals, and whales.

molars (MOH-lurz)
Low, flat teeth at the top
and bottom of a mammal's
mouth, behind the canine
teeth. Molars are used for
chewing and grinding
up food.

papillae (pah-PI-lee) Tiny
bumps on the upper side of
the tongue of humans and
other animals.

predator (PREH-duh-ter)
An animal that hunts and kills
other animals for food.

prey (PRAY) An animal that is hunted and killed for food by other animals.

pupil (PYOO-pul) An opening in the center of a person's or animal's eye through which light passes into the eye. The pupil becomes larger or smaller depending on how strong the surrounding light is.

radius (RAY-dee-us) The bone on the inner side of the lower part of an animal's front leg.

rodent (ROH-dent) One of many types of mammals that have two large front teeth they use to gnaw or nibble at food. Rats, mice, squirrels, and beavers are rodents. One third of all mammals are rodents.

rosette (roh-ZET) A round or circular dark marking on the coat of some animals. The center of a rosette is a lighter color.

savanna (suh-VA-nuh) A flat, grassy plain with some widely scattered trees. Savannas are in hot regions of the world, such as parts of Africa.

scapula (SKA-pyuh-luh) The triangular bone in each shoulder of a person or animal.

semidesert (seh-mee-DIH-zurt) A semidesert area is dry like a desert, but has some grass and other plants in it.

skeleton (SKEH-leh-tun) All the bones in a person's or animal's body.

solitary (SAH-leh-ter-ee) Living alone, and not as part of a group.

species (SPEE-sheez) Groups of animals that are similar in appearance and have many other features in common. Members of the same species mate to produce offspring.

stalking (STO-king) Quietly and secretly following a person or animal, while remaining hidden from sight.

stealth (STELTH) The ability to creep up close to prey without being seen or heard.

tropical (TRAH-puh-kul) Describes an area that is hot and close to the equator.

ulna (UL-nuh) The bone on the outer side of the lower part of an animal's front leg.

vegetation (veh-jih-TAY-shun) All the plant life, such as grasses, trees, and shrubs, in an area.

vertebrae (VER-tuh-bray) Small bones that form the backbone of a person or animal. Vertebrae point out sideways on each side of the spine.

Index

Websites

Due to the changing nature of Internet links, PowerKids Press has developed an online list of websites related to the subject of this book. This site is updated regularly. Please use this link to access the list:
www.powerkidslinks.com/disc/cats/